ELLIE SIMMONDS

Roy Apps

Illustrated by Chris King

First published in 2013 by
Franklin Watts
338 Euston Road
London NW1 3BH

Franklin Watts Australia
Level 17/207 Kent Street
Sydney NSW 2000

Text © Roy Apps 2013
Illustrations © Chris King 2013
Cover design by Peter Scoulding

A CIP catalogue record for this book
is available from the British Library.

ISBN: 978 1 4451 2231 1

1 3 5 7 9 10 8 6 4 2

Printed in Great Britain

Franklin Watts is a division of Hachette Children's Books,
an Hachette UK company.
www.hachette.co.uk

Chapter One:

A Hard Choice

"Come on, Blodwyn! Come on, girl!"
Ellie pushed her heels into the warm
flanks of the white pony. She gripped
the reins; the pony snorted, then began
to trot across the field.

Ellie had been given Blodwyn when she was eight years old, but she had been riding a lot longer. Blodwyn was a Welsh pony. She was small, but she was a perfect match for Ellie. At the stables, there were many bigger horses. Ellie enjoyed talking to them, feeding them and helping out.

As she turned Blodwyn round at the end of the field, she heard her mum calling her from the stable yard. Surely, it wasn't time to go in already? She slowed Blodwyn right down, to make the last bit of her ride last even longer.

When she reached the stable yard, she complained to her mum: "Can't I stay out longer? I've only been round the field a few times!"

"Blodwyn needs a good rub down," her mum replied. "Then she needs to be fed. And you've got to put all your tack away. It already looks as if you're going to be late for your swimming lesson again."

"Oh, Mum," Ellie groaned. She enjoyed swimming and she enjoyed riding, but sometimes there just didn't seem to be enough hours in the day to do both.

In the car, Ellie's mum looked at the clock on the dashboard. "Eleanor, we're going to be about 15 minutes late for your swimming and you still didn't have time to rub Blodwyn down properly," she said with a sigh.

Ellie stared straight ahead, out of the windscreen. Ellie's mum always called her by her full name, Eleanor — although all her friends called her Ellie.

"It's good that you've got your hobbies," Ellie's mum went on, "but you really haven't got the time to do both riding and swimming. You've got to make a choice, Eleanor. Riding or swimming. Which one is it going to be?"

Chapter Two:

The Choice is Made

Ellie lay awake in her bed unable to sleep. She kept thinking about the choice she had to make: riding or swimming. Deep down though, she already knew the answer. In fact, she'd always known what the answer would be. She loved riding Blodwyn, but for Ellie, swimming was something very special.

The Simmonds had a pool in their garden. Ellie couldn't remember a time when she hadn't enjoyed being in the water. When she was younger, it had seemed that most of her time had been spent with friends in the garden pool. Now Ellie swam most days with her friends at the big pool in town.

She loved the coolness of the water when she first dived in, and the waves as she splashed and sped along. Riding was something to do on your own, but swimming was something to be enjoyed with friends.

Ellie had entered her first swimming gala when she was eight. The thrill of competing against other swimmers was fantastic. She came last in that race, but she continued to take part in galas and competitions. Although Ellie wasn't winning, she was selected to take part in World Class Talent, a training programme for young, talented athletes.

While Ellie was away at one of the programme's summer camps, a coach took Ellie to one side.

"You've got a real talent, you know," she said.

"Have I?" asked Ellie. "I don't seem to win anything."

"That's because you're competing with able-bodied swimmers, who are all twice your size," replied the coach. "I've got some timings here that show just how well you would do if you were competing against swimmers with a similar disability to yours." She laid out a spreadsheet on the table that was in front of them. "These are the timings you've managed this weekend, Ellie," she said. "You're doing the same timings as an 18-year-old swimmer with disabilities."

Ellie gasped. "Really?"

The coach nodded. "And how old are you?"

"Nine," replied Ellie.

In the summer of 2004, Ellie skipped a few of her swimming lessons. Instead, she sat glued to the television watching the Athens Paralympic Games.

"That's what I want to do," she declared.

Ellie had a dream: to become a Paralympic swimmer.

Chapter Three:
Surprises

Ellie entered her first gala for swimmers with a disability when she was just ten years old. There were plenty of surprises for her, the first was that there were swimmers with so many different types of disability.

One of the organisers told Ellie about the disability classification system.

"You're classified on a physical disability scale from S1 to S10," he explained. "The S stands for swimming. The most disabled swimmers are S1 and the least disabled swimmers are S10." Ellie was classified as S6.

The second surprise for Ellie was finding herself listed to take part in races against swimmers who were less or more disabled than she was.

"You don't have to worry about that," said the organiser of the gala. "From now on the important thing is your time. Every disabled swimmer gets points based on the world record for a particular classification. We need to see what kind of time you can set compared to the S6 world records."

But the biggest surprise of all was that a number of the competitors seemed familiar to Ellie.

"I think I've seen some of those swimmers before," Ellie said to her mum, in a puzzled voice.

"You have. On the television, taking part in the Athens Paralympic Games!"

Ellie was amazed that she was swimming at the same gala as Nyree Lewis, who was also classified as S6, and who had won gold at the Athens Paralympics.

Ellie didn't win anything at her first swimming gala, but a few months later she went to the British Junior Championships. There, in spite of being the youngest competitor, she won all her races in the under-14 category. She also won the trophy for the best performance at the championships!

Ellie had proved herself a winner. She
was on her way.

The following year, when she was
eleven, Ellie was away at summer
camp. One morning, the camp warden
came rushing over to her.

"Ellie!" he called. "Your mum's just been on the phone. She wants you to ring her as soon as possible. She's got some news."

"Good news?" asked Ellie, a little worried.

The camp warden nodded. "Judging by the tone of her voice, it sounded like very good news indeed."

Ellie rang her mum, all the time wondering what the news could be. When she got through, her mum was almost too excited to speak. Eventually she said: "Eleanor! You've been selected for the 2006 Swimming World Championships in Durban. You're going to South Africa!"

Chapter Four:

Saying Goodbye

Ellie was thrilled to be going to South Africa. The World Championships lasted just over a week, but Ellie and the team spent three weeks in Durban before the start of the competition to train and get used to the hot climate.

Ellie enjoyed being part of the British team. She was still only 12 years old — the next youngest person in the team was 15. When it came to the competition itself, Ellie swam personal best times in every event she entered. She loved the beaches and the sunshine of Durban so much — she didn't really want to go home!

Coming back to swimming lessons in England was a bit of a shock. Ellie had been training with competitive swimmers for a month. She had forgotten what it was like trying to train in a pool full of noisy children. Then and there she knew that if she was going to pursue her dream of becoming a top swimmer, she would need to find a new swimming club.

Ellie and her mum and dad talked about what she should do. They found out that there was a swimming coach in Wales who specialised in working with swimmers in Ellie's S6 classification. His name was Billy Pye. So they drove down to Swansea to see him.

After the meeting with Billy, on the long journey home in the car, Ellie's mum said: "Well, Eleanor, what you think?"

"We got on really well," replied Ellie. "I think he could help me a lot. But…"

"But what?" asked Ellie's mum.

"We'd have to move house, wouldn't we?"

Ellie's mum nodded. "Yes."

"Suppose it didn't work out? Suppose I hated living in Wales? And I'd miss all my friends!" Suddenly, she felt very scared and very confused. "Oh, I don't know what to do!"

"It's got to be your decision, Eleanor," said her mum, quietly. "I suppose the question is, just how important to you is your dream of becoming a world-class swimmer?"

Ellie knew there was only one answer to that question.

At the end of the summer term, she said goodbye to all of her friends at

school. It was hard, and there were lots of tears, but Ellie knew that it was what she had to do.

Chapter Five:
Beijing

Swimming under Billy's new routine was tough. Ellie trained four mornings a week in the pool, from six o'clock until half-past seven. After school she trained from half-past three to half-past five.

On Saturdays she swam for two hours,
from seven o'clock to nine o'clock.
After that, Ellie and her mum drove
back to the West Midlands for the rest
of the weekend. She had Sundays off —
but she still had to do her school work!

The hard work was worth it. At the
trials for the 2008 Beijing Paralympics,
Ellie won the S6 400 metres freestyle
in a world record-breaking time!

With that sort of achievement, she was guaranteed a place in the British Paralympic team.

Just as in the World Championships in Durban, Ellie found herself the youngest member of the team. Not only that, she was the youngest British athlete in the whole of the Beijing Paralympics!

Ellie spent a lot of time with the Team GB coaches, looking at every aspect of her swimming: starts, turns, finishes; everything had to be as good as possible.

The first race Ellie was in at the Beijing Paralympics was the S6 200 metres individual medley — in which all four swimming strokes are used. It was a race Ellie hoped to get a medal in.

She stood at the side of the pool waiting for the race to start. She adjusted her goggles. She fidgeted. She adjusted her goggles again. Suddenly, she felt overcome with nerves. She couldn't get the thought out of her head that here she was, just 13 years old, competing at the Beijing Paralympics against athletes who were all much older then she was.

She thought to herself, "Once I'm in the pool, I'll be able to focus." But she couldn't. She didn't get into her rhythm at all. She didn't win a medal.

A few days later, Ellie was swimming again, this time in the S6 100 metres freestyle. As the swimmers powered through the water, Ellie knew it was a very close race. They approached the finish with hardly anything between the swimmers as they went to touch the wall. Ellie gave it one, final push.

The race was over. Ellie pushed her goggles up to look at the scoreboard. It took a second or two for her to see that not only had she won a medal, she had won gold! Ellie burst into tears of joy. Television cameras captured the special moment for the whole world to see.

Just a few days afterwards, Ellie was back on the winners' podium again after winning gold in the S6 400 metres freestyle.

As she waved to the crowd she really felt on top of the world.

Chapter Six:

Ups and Downs

When Ellie got back from Beijing, she suddenly found she was famous. People in the street came up to her and said things like:

"You're that swimmer, aren't you? I saw

you on the telly!"

On the first day of the new school term, Ellie's school sent a limousine to pick her up.

When she arrived, the whole school was waiting for her outside. Ellie showed everyone her Paralympic medals. Then the headteacher said: "Would you like to say a few words, Ellie?"

Ellie gulped. "What, like a speech, do you mean?" she asked, horrified.

"Tell us what it was like at the Paralympics," the headteacher suggested.

So Ellie did. She felt really embarrassed, but when she had finished, everyone cheered.

There was more cheering later on in the year when Ellie went to London to receive the BBC Young Sports Personality of the Year Award 2008. It was presented to her by Ricky Hatton and Theo Walcott. It was very exciting, until she realised she had to give a speech — again! Then it was suddenly nerve-wracking and embarrassing.

One day, Ellie got a letter. It was about some sort of appointment, but she couldn't make much sense of it, so she put it on the kitchen table and went off to school. When she got home, her mum said: "Is this letter yours, Eleanor?"

Ellie nodded.

"Well, if you don't want it, put it in the recycling. Who's it from, anyway?"

"I don't know," said Ellie. "Something about an appointment."

Ellie's mum read the letter. Then she went pale and started muttering: "Oh my goodness!"

"What is it, Mum?" asked Ellie.

"You've been appointed a Member of the Order of the British Empire," replied her mum. "You're going to be an MBE!"

Weeks later Ellie travelled to London and was presented with her MBE by the Queen at Buckingham Palace. Ellie was the youngest person ever to have received the honour.

After all the excitement died down,
things returned to normal very quickly.
Swimming, school, swimming. It was as
if Beijing had never happened. Ellie felt
very low. She felt she had nothing to
look forward to.

Then one day, Billy, her coach, said:
"Fun time is over! The real hard work
starts here. I think you should increase

your training hours."

Ellie sighed. "What for?"

"The next Paralympics, of course!" exclaimed Billy. "London 2012. You've got just three-and-a-half years to prepare!"

Chapter Seven:

London 2012

Ellie trained hard and won gold at the 2009 IPC — International Paralympic Committee — European Championships, the 2009 IPC World Championships and the 2010 Paralympic World Cup.

Ellie knew that London 2012 would be different to Beijing, though. When she'd gone to Beijing, nobody had heard of her. Now she was a double Paralympic gold medal winner. She had been in the newspapers and on TV; she was even an MBE. Everyone would be expecting her to do well in front of her home crowd. This time, there would be other swimmers who weren't around in 2008, coming through to challenge her.

London was different for another reason, too. Ellie had media work to do: modelling the Team GB swimwear, doing newspaper interviews, appearing on TV. All the time though, she made sure to focus on her training for the games.

As she stood at the edge of the pool, waiting to start the S6 400 metre freestyle final, Ellie looked round at the other swimmers. Back in the Olympic Village they were all good mates, but

she knew that once the race started, it
would be war.

She fiddled with her goggles. She
fidgeted. She was nervous. Would it
be like her first race in Beijing all over
again? She began to panic. Would nerves
get the better of her?

From the start of the race the American swimmer Victoria Arlen was out in front. Victoria was Ellie's great rival, and the current S6 400 metre world record holder. Ellie stayed with Victoria, but there seemed to be no way she could push in front. Then, on the final turn, Ellie edged into the lead. From somewhere deep down inside her, she found the strength to power past her rival in the last 50 metres. She touched the wall 0.61 seconds in front. She had won gold!

As Ellie held on to the side of the pool and pushed up her goggles, the Aquatics Centre echoed wildly as the crowd cheered. Tears came into her eyes. This was the first of four medals — two gold, one silver and one bronze — which she would go on to win at the London Paralympic Games.

On the podium, Ellie joined in with

the crowd as they sang the National Anthem. For Ellie, it was the best moment ever. She knew that it was one she would remember for the rest of her life.

Fact file
Ellie Simmonds

Full name: Eleanor Simmonds

Nickname: Ellie

Born: 11 November 1994, Walsall, England

Height: 1.23 metres

Major Medals

- **2008 Paralympic Games (Beijing)**
  Gold, S6 100m Freestyle
  Gold, S6 400m Freestyle

- **2009 IPC Swimming World Championships 25m (Rio de Janeiro)**
  Gold, S6 100m Freestyle, S6 400m Freestyle,
  S6 200m Individual Medley, S6 50m Freestyle

- **2010 IPC Swimming World Championships (Eindhoven)**
  Gold, S6 100m Freestyle, S6 400m Freestyle,
  S6 200m Individual Medley, S6 50m Freestyle
- **2010 Paralympic World Cup (Manchester)**
  Gold, S6 25m Individual Medley

- **2011 Paralympic World Cup**
  Gold, S6 200m Individual Medley
- **2011 IPC Swimming European Championships**
  Gold, S6 200m Individual Medley
  Gold, S6 400m Freestyle

- **2012 Paralympic Games (London)**
  Gold, S6 400m Freestyle
  Gold, S6 200m Individual Medley
  Silver, S6 100m Freestyle
  Bronze, S6 50m Freestyle

Honours

- **2008** BBC Young Sports Personality of the Year.
- **2009** Appointed a Member of the Order of the British Empire (MBE).
- **2011** Jaguar Academy of Sport Awards: Best British Sporting Performance for an Athlete with Disability.
- **2013** Appointed an Officer of the Order of the British Empire (OBE).

Further information

IPC Classification in Disability Sport

Classification is a way of organising competition in sport.

In sports, such as boxing, golf and weightlifting, all athletes are classified. So, for example, in boxing you have lightweight, welterweight and heavyweight classes.

In disability sport, athletes are classified according to their impairments. You need different skills and abilities for different sports, so each sport has its own specific International Paralympic Committee classification rules.

In swimming, athletes with a physical disability are classified between S1 and S10, with S1 being the most severely disabled and S10 being the least severely disabled. To find out more, visit:

**www.paralympic.org/
Classification/Introduction**

About Ellie

Ellie has Achondroplasia, a bone growth disorder which causes dwarfism. To find out more about her, and to get all her latest news, visit:

www.elliesimmonds.com